LIFE'S LITTLE BOOK OF WISDOM
FUN FACTS FOR SPORTS LOVERS

10669811

© 2009 by Barbour Publishing, Inc.

Compiled by Lee Warren.

ISBN 978-1-60260-472-8

Published by Barbour Publishing, Inc., P.O. Box 719, Uhrichsville, Ohio 44683
www.barbourbooks.com

Our mission is to publish and distribute inspirational products offering exceptional value and biblical encouragement to the masses.

Member of the
Evangelical Christian
Publishers Association

Printed in the United States of America.

Life's Little Book of Wisdom

Fun Facts for Sports Lovers

BARBOUR
PUBLISHING

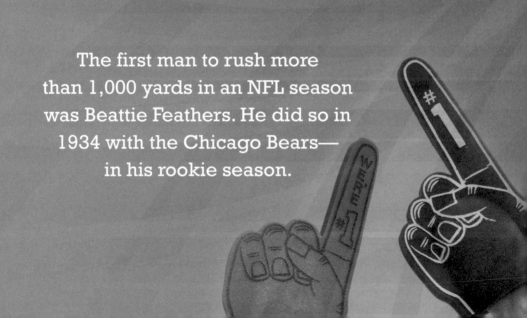

The first man to rush more
than 1,000 yards in an NFL season
was Beattie Feathers. He did so in
1934 with the Chicago Bears—
in his rookie season.

A baseball has 108 stitches.

Wilt Chamberlain played 1,045 games in the NBA— and never fouled out.

At the age of 102, Elsie McLean became the oldest person ever to make a hole-in-one on a regulation golf course. She used a driver on a par three, 100-yard hole.

Steffi Graf is the only player, male or female, to win all four major tennis tournaments at least four times.

In 1959, Lee Petty won NASCAR's inaugural Daytona 500, winning $19,050. Today, drivers earn more than $1.5 million for coming in first.

In the 1924 Olympics,
Eric Liddell refused to compete in the
100-meter event—his best event—
because it was held on a Sunday.
He chose another event—
the 400-meter race—
and still won gold.

Only two days a year have no major professional sports on the schedule: the day before and the day after the Major League Baseball All-Star game.

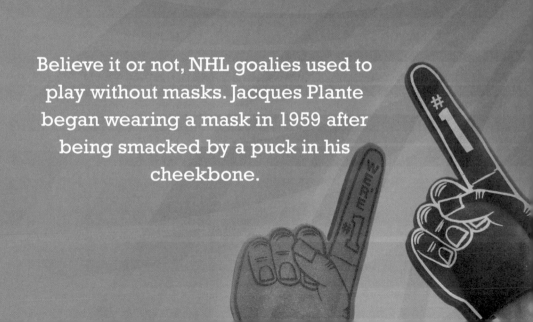

Believe it or not, NHL goalies used to play without masks. Jacques Plante began wearing a mask in 1959 after being smacked by a puck in his cheekbone.

Do you not know that in a race
all the runners run, but only one receives the
prize? So run that you may obtain it.

1 CORINTHIANS 9:24

Tiger Woods was born with the first name of Eldrick. "Tiger" was a nickname in honor of a South Vietnamese soldier who had fought courageously alongside Woods' father.

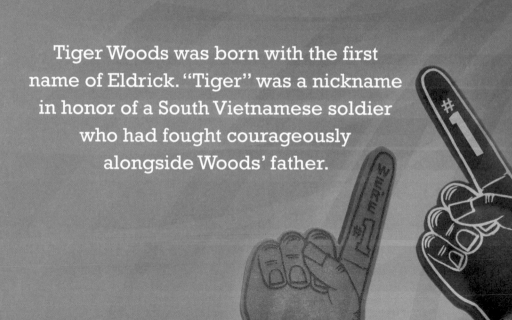

The first official basketball game was played in 1892 at the Springfield, Massachusetts, YMCA. The nine-player teams used a soccer ball and peach baskets nailed to a balcony.

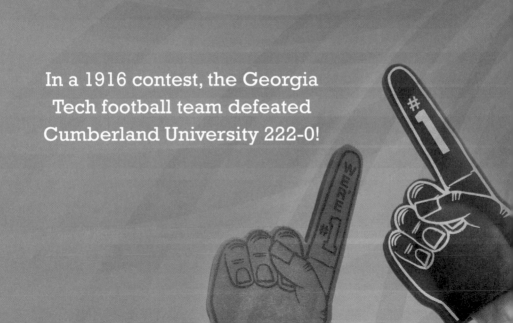

In a 1916 contest, the Georgia Tech football team defeated Cumberland University 222-0!

The word *hockey* is believed to come from the French word *hoquet* which means "shepherd's crook" or "bent stick."

According to Detroit's official website, the Motor City has the most registered bowlers in the United States.

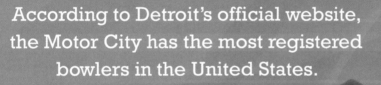

In a 2005 tennis tournament in Rome, Andy Roddick overruled a judge's call on triple match point, allowing his opponent, Fernando Verdasco back into the game. Verdasco rallied to win the match—but Roddick won fans' respect.

The route for the Tour de France changes every year, but is always approximately 3,500 kilometers (2,175 miles).

The world's best Ping-Pong players can
hit the ball more than 100 miles per hour.

Pittsburgh is the only U.S. city in which at least three of its major sports teams wear the same colors: black and gold.

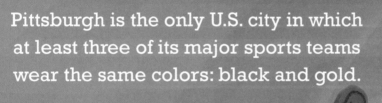

And whatever you do, in word or deed,
do everything in the name of the Lord Jesus,
giving thanks to God the Father through him.

Colossians 3:17

Every year, Slazenger sends 42,000 tennis balls to Wimbledon: 15,000 for practice, 21,600 for tournament play, and 5,400 as backups.

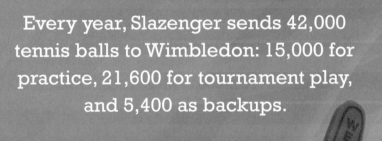

NASCAR pioneer Tim Flock raced nine times with a monkey named Jocko Flocko in his car. During a 1953 race, Jocko got loose and Flock had to make a pit stop—causing him to lose the lead and finish second.

The Stanley Cup, awarded to the best team in hockey since 1893, was originally only seven and a half inches high. Today, it's approximately thirty-five inches high and weighs about thirty-five pounds.

The first college football game took place
on November 6, 1869, with Rutgers
University defeating Princeton 6–4.

In 1976, a baseball game in the Houston Astrodome was actually rained out—because flooded streets nearby prevented umpires and fans from reaching the stadium.

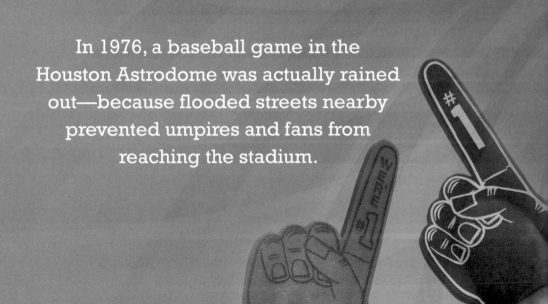

The five Olympic rings represent five continents linked together in friendship.

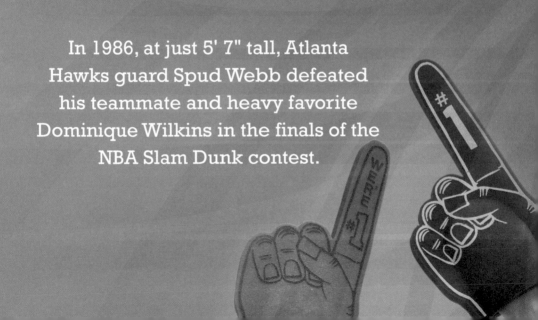

In 1986, at just 5' 7" tall, Atlanta Hawks guard Spud Webb defeated his teammate and heavy favorite Dominique Wilkins in the finals of the NBA Slam Dunk contest.

The Olympic torch that runners carry around the world is thirty-three inches long and weighs about three pounds. It's made of silver, copper, and glass.

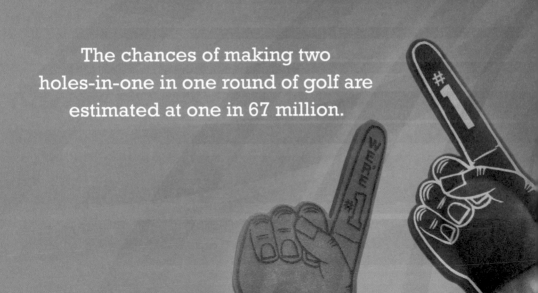

The chances of making two holes-in-one in one round of golf are estimated at one in 67 million.

So, whether you eat or drink, or whatever you do,
do all to the glory of God.

1 Corinthians 10:31

The Cincinnati Reds were the first major league team to travel by airplane, for a series in Chicago in 1934. Twelve years later, the New York Yankees became the first team to fly on a regular basis.

NASCAR drivers traversing a straightaway at 200 miles per hour cover 293 feet per second—nearly the length of a football field.

William "Pudge" Heffelfinger was the first person paid to play football. In 1892, he received five hundred dollars to play a game for the Allegheny Athletic Association.

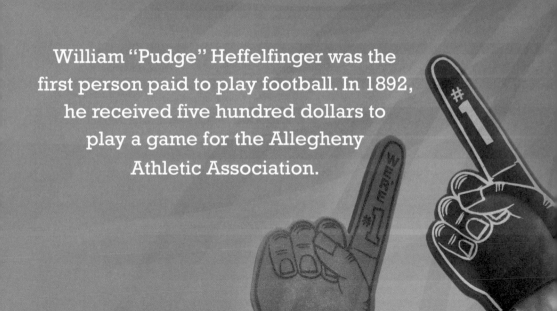

In 1999, the National Collegiate Athletic Association began awarding the NCAA Sportsmanship Award to athletes who best demonstrate fairness, civility, honesty, unselfishness, respect, and responsibility in the game.

Arnold Palmer was the first golfer
to win the Masters four times
(in 1958, 1960, 1962, and 1964).

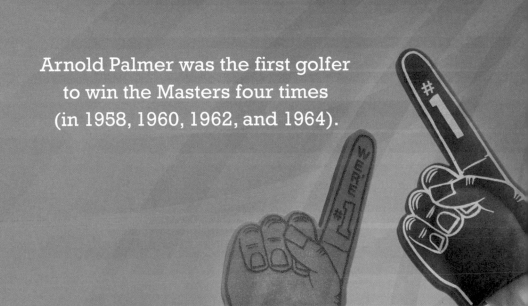

Pete Sampras is the youngest tennis player to win the United States Open. He was 19 when he took the title in 1990.

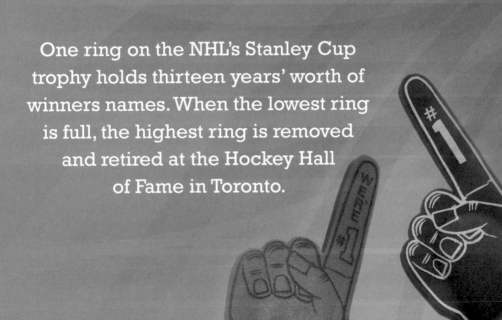

One ring on the NHL's Stanley Cup trophy holds thirteen years' worth of winners names. When the lowest ring is full, the highest ring is removed and retired at the Hockey Hall of Fame in Toronto.

In a 2006 basketball game in Rochester, New York, an autistic team manager, Jason McElwain, got a chance to play the final four minutes of his team's last game of the season— and sank seven shots for 20 points.

Volleyball was originally called *mintonette,* but the name was later changed due to the way players volleyed the ball back and forth.

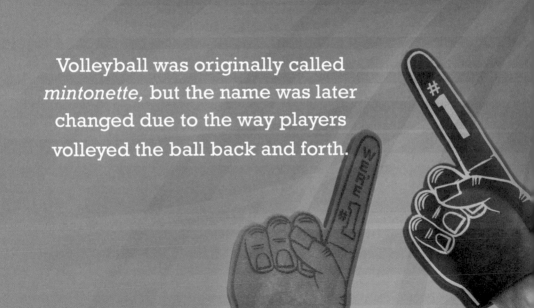

An athlete is not crowned unless he competes according to the rules.

2 TIMOTHY 2:5

The value of a touchdown was changed from four points to five in 1898.

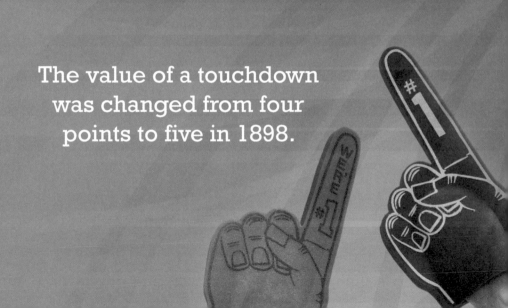

As a member of the 1973 Oakland A's,
Darold Knowles became the only pitcher ever to
appear in all seven games of a World Series.

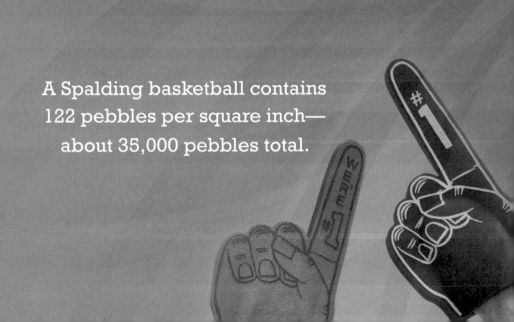

A Spalding basketball contains 122 pebbles per square inch— about 35,000 pebbles total.

Beverly Hanson won the first ever Ladies
Professional Golf Association (LPGA)
Championship in 1955.

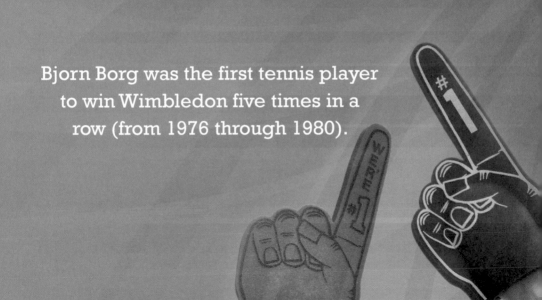

Bjorn Borg was the first tennis player to win Wimbledon five times in a row (from 1976 through 1980).

The heart rate of NASCAR drivers ranges from 120 to 150 beats per minute over the course of a race—about the same rate as a marathon runner.

The last year that Olympic gold medals were made of solid gold: 1912.

Football's forward pass was legalized in 1906. George Parratt, who played for Massillon, Ohio, completed the first one to Dan Riley on October 27 of that year.

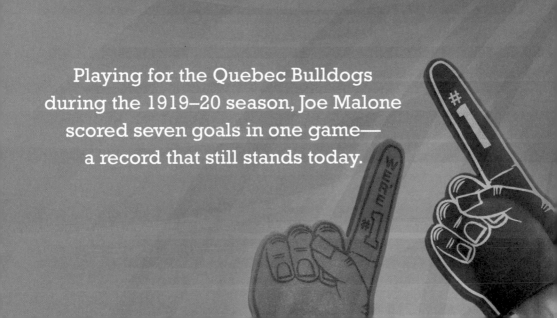

Playing for the Quebec Bulldogs during the 1919–20 season, Joe Malone scored seven goals in one game— a record that still stands today.

Do nothing from rivalry or conceit, but in humility count others more significant than yourselves.

PHILIPPIANS 2:3

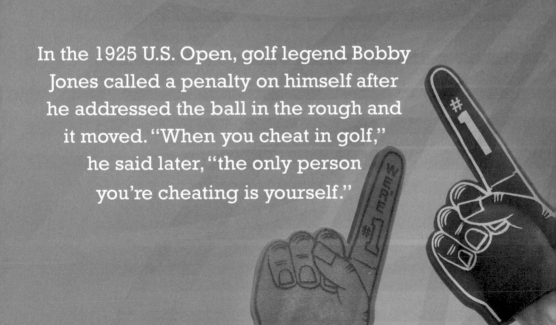

In the 1925 U.S. Open, golf legend Bobby Jones called a penalty on himself after he addressed the ball in the rough and it moved. "When you cheat in golf," he said later, "the only person you're cheating is yourself."

The average NBA player is 6 feet,
7 inches tall and weighs 224 pounds.

In 1904, football rule makers changed field goals from five points to four.

The Edmonton Oilers' Wayne Gretzky set
the NHL record during the 1981–82
season when he scored 92 goals.

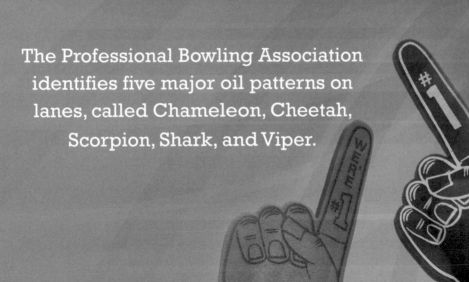

The Professional Bowling Association identifies five major oil patterns on lanes, called Chameleon, Cheetah, Scorpion, Shark, and Viper.

Former tennis star Michael Chang's family started the Christian Sports League (CSL) to work with local churches to share the Gospel through organized and competitive sports.

The first year that the Olympics were fully covered on American television: 1960. CBS cameras captured the events in Rome and the tape was flown to New York City each day.

The Boston Marathon is the world's oldest annual marathon, with more than twenty-thousand participants every year.

The 1899 Cleveland Spiders claim the worst record in Major League Baseball history at 20–134 (for a .150 winning percentage). The team was defunct the next season.

I have fought the good fight, I have finished the race, I have kept the faith.

2 Timothy 4:7

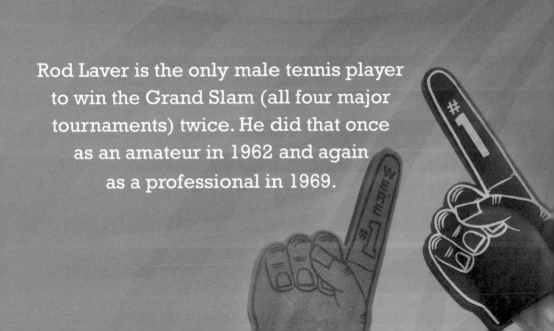

Rod Laver is the only male tennis player to win the Grand Slam (all four major tournaments) twice. He did that once as an amateur in 1962 and again as a professional in 1969.

Temperatures inside a stock car can climb
as high as 170 degrees near the floorboards.

The longest game in NHL history occurred in 1936 when the Detroit Red Wings and the Montreal Maroons battled into a sixth overtime period, playing the equivalent of nearly three full games. Detroit won, 1–0.

In 1909, the point value of a football field goal was changed from four points to three.

Baseball's first World Series was played in 1903, a best-of-nine series between the Boston Americans (later the Red Sox) and the Pittsburgh Pirates. Boston won the series, five games to three.

Snowboarding became an official Olympic event
in 1998. Competitors take part in two events:
the half-pipe and the giant slalom.

When thirteen-year-old Natalie Gilbert,
selected to sing the National Anthem
before a 2003 NBA playoff game,
forgot the words partway into the song,
Portland Trailblazers' coach Maurice
Cheeks quickly joined her on court,
put his arm around her,
and helped her finish the song.

In 1911, Ray Harroun won the first Indianapolis 500, averaging slightly under 75 miles per hour. Recent winners have averaged between 138 mph and 167 mph.

During an LPGA tournament in Ohio, Meg Mallon hit a ball that wobbled on the edge of the cup for some time before dropping in. She scored the stroke but was later disqualified for not taking a penalty stroke for waiting more than ten seconds to hit the ball into the hole.

For the moment all discipline seems painful
rather than pleasant, but later it yields
the peaceful fruit of righteousness to
those who have been trained by it.

HEBREWS 12:11

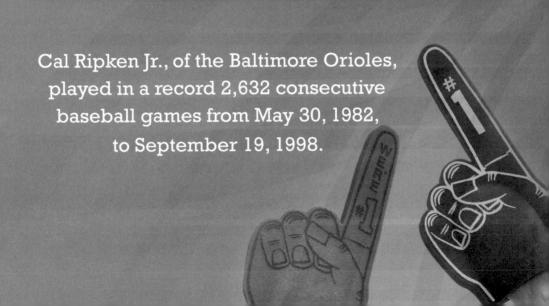

Cal Ripken Jr., of the Baltimore Orioles, played in a record 2,632 consecutive baseball games from May 30, 1982, to September 19, 1998.

Richard Petty won 200 races during his NASCAR career, nearly twice as many as the second-place driver, David Pearson (with 105 wins).

In 1943, with many players serving in World War II, the Pittsburgh Steelers and Philadelphia Eagles merged into one team. The "Steagles," as they were called, went 5–4–1 for the season.

The World Cup, held every four years in a different country, is the biggest soccer tournament in the world with billions of viewers globally.

Professional golfer Kathy Whitworth won 88 tournaments in her career, more than any other golfer, male or female.

In 1997, sixteen-year-old Martina Hingis became the youngest female tennis player to be ranked number one in the world since the ranking system began.

Bernie Geoffrion is credited with introducing the slap shot to the NHL in 1951. He was nicknamed "Boom Boom" for the way he struck the puck.

After the 1948–49 season, the National Basketball League (NBL) and the Basketball Association of America (BAA) merged to become the National Basketball Association (NBA).

The NFL's Tampa Bay Buccaneers lost their first 26 games. During their inaugural season (1976), the Bucs were 0–14. Then they lost their first twelve games of 1977 before finally posting a W.

For you were bought with a price.
So glorify God in your body.

1 CORINTHIANS 6:20

In 1941, Joe DiMaggio hit safely in 56 consecutive games—a major league record that still stands.

Nolan Ryan threw a record seven no-hitters in his Major League career, the first one in 1973 against Kansas City, the last in 1991 against Toronto.

Four teams from the defunct American Basketball Association (1967–1976) survive in today's NBA: Indiana, Denver, New York, and San Antonio.

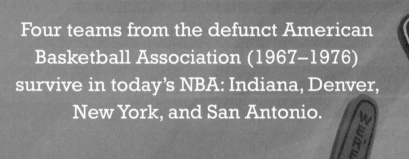

The youngest known golfer to make a
hole-in-one: Coby Orr. The five-year-old
used a five-iron to ace a 103-yard hole
on a San Antonio course in 1975.

Three female tennis players have won the Grand Slam (all four major tournaments in one year): Maureen Connolly, 1953; Margaret Smith Court, 1970; and Steffi Graf, 1988. Graf also won the Olympic gold medal that year.

On his twentieth attempt, Dale Earnhardt finally won the Daytona 500 in 1998. Crews from every team lined up on pit road to congratulate him after the race.

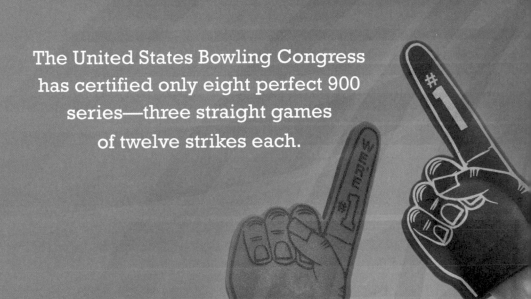

The United States Bowling Congress has certified only eight perfect 900 series—three straight games of twelve strikes each.

In 1985, Dirk Borgognone of Reno, Nevada, kicked the longest field goal in high school football history—68 yards.

In 1976, Toronto Maple Leaf Darryl Sittler scored ten points (six goals, four assists) in an NHL game against the Boston Bruins.

So I do not run aimlessly;
I do not box as one beating the air.

1 CORINTHIANS 9:26

Some 90 percent of the balls on the USGA's "Conforming Ball List" have between 300 and 450 dimples. Those dimples help the ball spin and create lift.

In 1962, against New York, Philadelphia's Wilt Chamberlain scored 100 points in an NBA game—a record that still stands today.

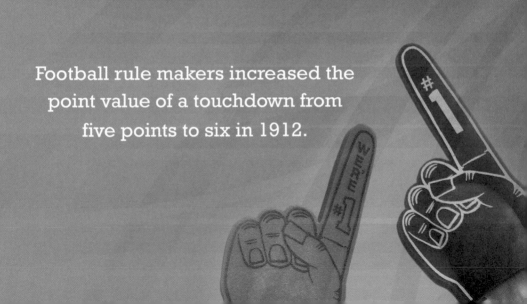

Football rule makers increased the point value of a touchdown from five points to six in 1912.

The National Hockey League was born in 1917—made up of the Montreal Canadiens, Montreal Wanderers, Ottawa Senators, Toronto Arenas, and Quebec Bulldogs.

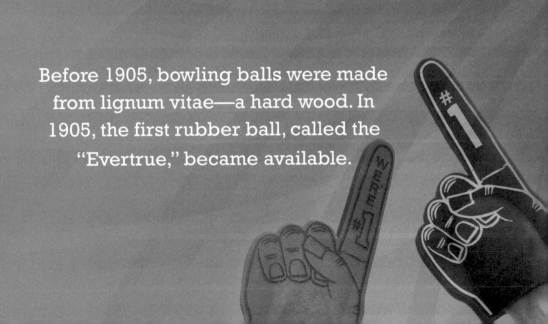

Before 1905, bowling balls were made from lignum vitae—a hard wood. In 1905, the first rubber ball, called the "Evertrue," became available.

In 1932, Henry "Bunny" Austin shocked the Queen of England by becoming the first player to wear shorts at Wimbledon.

Volleyball features five types of serve: the basic underarm, the overarm float, the overarm topspin, the roundhouse, and the jump serve.

NASCAR driver David Reutimann sports a cross decal on his car. He says it gives him a chance to talk to people about his faith in Christ.

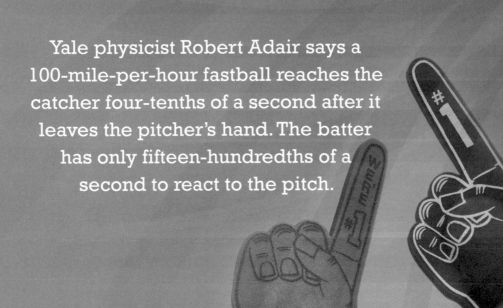

Yale physicist Robert Adair says a 100-mile-per-hour fastball reaches the catcher four-tenths of a second after it leaves the pitcher's hand. The batter has only fifteen-hundredths of a second to react to the pitch.

I was pushed hard, so that I was falling,
but the LORD helped me.

PSALM 118:13

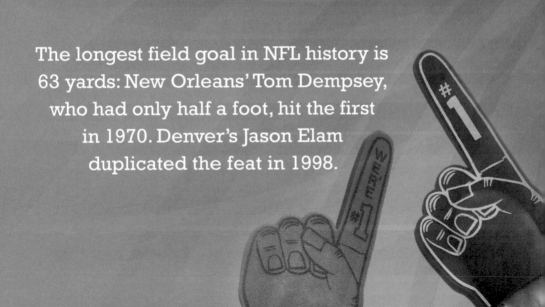

The longest field goal in NFL history is 63 yards: New Orleans' Tom Dempsey, who had only half a foot, hit the first in 1970. Denver's Jason Elam duplicated the feat in 1998.

The only pitcher to ever throw a perfect game in the World Series: the Yankees' Don Larsen. He did it in Game 5 of the 1956 fall classic against Brooklyn.

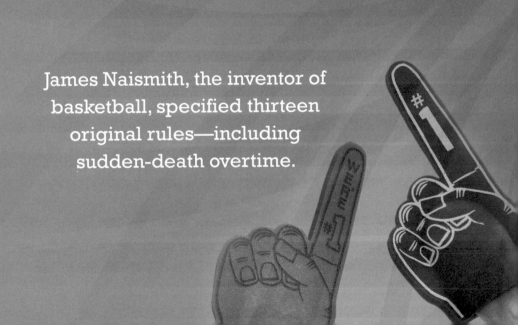

James Naismith, the inventor of basketball, specified thirteen original rules—including sudden-death overtime.

The first U.S. Open golf tournament was held in Newport, Rhode Island, in 1895 with ten professionals and one amateur competing. Horace Rawlins won.

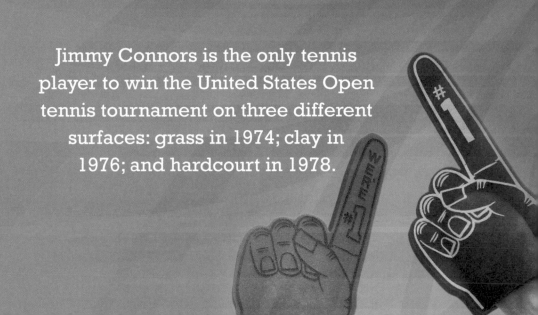

Jimmy Connors is the only tennis player to win the United States Open tennis tournament on three different surfaces: grass in 1974; clay in 1976; and hardcourt in 1978.

NASCAR drivers can lose five to ten pounds in sweat during a race.

The ancient Olympic games began in 776 BC. The first "modern" Olympics were held in Athens in 1896.

The first nationally broadcast NFL game: the Thanksgiving Day, 1934, contest between the Chicago Bears and Detroit Lions on NBC radio.

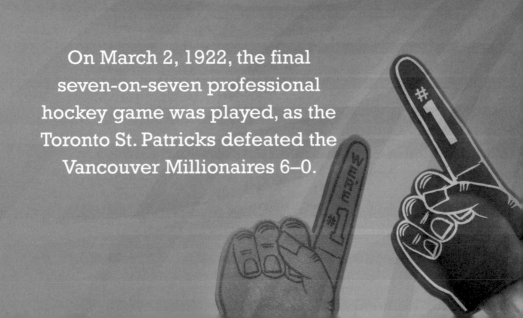

On March 2, 1922, the final seven-on-seven professional hockey game was played, as the Toronto St. Patricks defeated the Vancouver Millionaires 6–0.

Every athlete exercises self-control in all things.

1 Corinthians 9:25

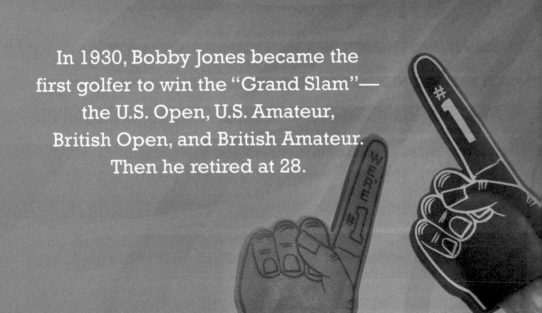

In 1930, Bobby Jones became the first golfer to win the "Grand Slam"— the U.S. Open, U.S. Amateur, British Open, and British Amateur. Then he retired at 28.

One of James Naismith's original thirteen rules of basketball: Players showing "evident intent" to injure another were to be ejected, with no substitution allowed.

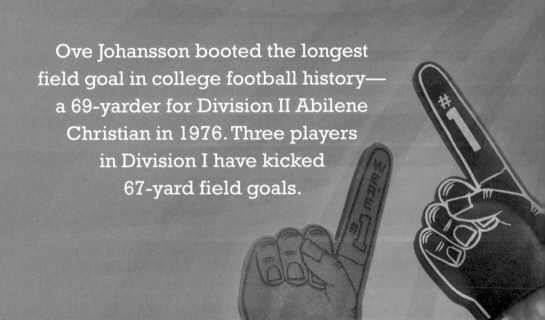

Ove Johansson booted the longest field goal in college football history— a 69-yarder for Division II Abilene Christian in 1976. Three players in Division I have kicked 67-yard field goals.

The first hockey game televised in the United States took place on February 25, 1940, as the New York Rangers faced the Montreal Canadiens. A single camera captured the Rangers' 6–2 victory for three hundred television receivers in the Big Apple.

An estimated ninety-five million people in more than ninety countries enjoy the sport of bowling.

The tennis term *love* (zero) originated
from the French word for "egg"—*l'ouef.*

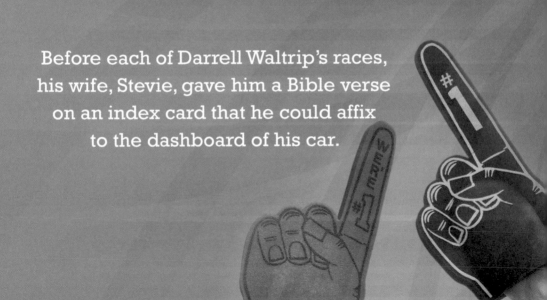

Before each of Darrell Waltrip's races, his wife, Stevie, gave him a Bible verse on an index card that he could affix to the dashboard of his car.

In the 1900 Olympic games, a Dutch rowing team replaced their coxswain with a 73-pound boy off the streets of Paris. They won the gold medal, but the boy disappeared before anything more could be discovered about him.

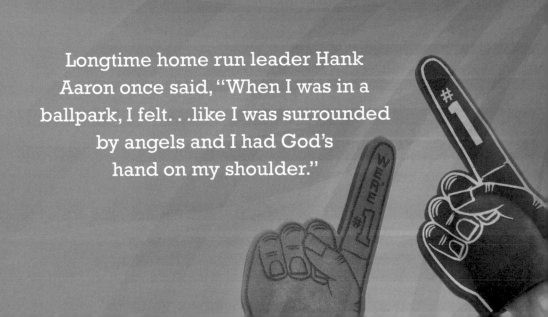

Longtime home run leader Hank Aaron once said, "When I was in a ballpark, I felt...like I was surrounded by angels and I had God's hand on my shoulder."

A man without self-control is like a city
broken into and left without walls.

PROVERBS 25:28

Some believe tennis is rooted in a game that was played in twelfth-century France, in which participants used their bare hands.

NASCAR drivers can experience as much as
3 Gs of force when making turns—comparable
to what space shuttle astronauts feel at liftoff.

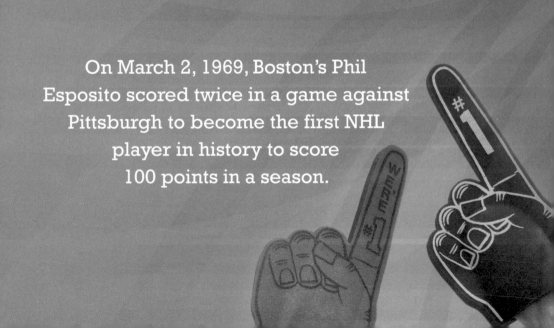

On March 2, 1969, Boston's Phil Esposito scored twice in a game against Pittsburgh to become the first NHL player in history to score 100 points in a season.

Along with his wife, NFL quarterback Kurt Warner founded the First Things First Foundation in 2001 to help children in need. The organization promotes the concept of putting faith and family first.

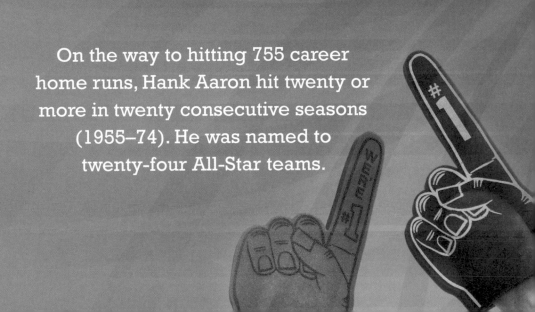

On the way to hitting 755 career home runs, Hank Aaron hit twenty or more in twenty consecutive seasons (1955–74). He was named to twenty-four All-Star teams.

The Olympic motto is *Citius, Altius, Fortius,*
Latin for, "Faster, Higher, Stronger."

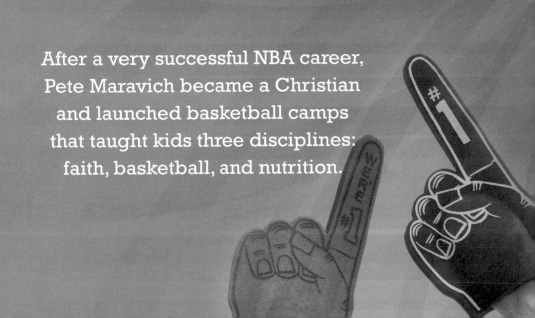

After a very successful NBA career,
Pete Maravich became a Christian
and launched basketball camps
that taught kids three disciplines:
faith, basketball, and nutrition.

During a 62-mile cycling race in the 1896 Olympics, Frenchman Leon Flameng politely stopped and waited while one of his competitors dealt with mechanical problems. Flameng still went on to win the gold medal.

Sam Snead sits atop the all-time career PGA Tour winners' list with 82.

Whoever sows sparingly will also reap sparingly, and whoever sows bountifully will also reap bountifully.

2 Corinthians 9:6

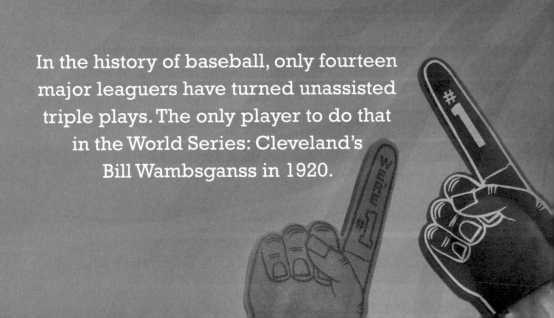

In the history of baseball, only fourteen major leaguers have turned unassisted triple plays. The only player to do that in the World Series: Cleveland's Bill Wambsganss in 1920.

The Daytona 500 was first televised
live in its entirety in 1979.

In 2002, an Ohio high school football coach encouraged his team to allow a mentally handicapped opposing player to score a touchdown on the final play of the game. They did, cheering him on for his 49-yard run.

In April 2008, Danica Patrick became
the first woman to win an IndyCar race,
taking first in the Indy Japan 300.

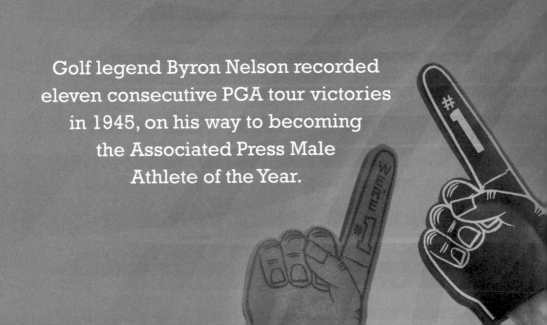

Golf legend Byron Nelson recorded
eleven consecutive PGA tour victories
in 1945, on his way to becoming
the Associated Press Male
Athlete of the Year.

In 1988, the Australian Open tennis tournament became the first tournament with a retractable roof over its center court. The stadium, located in Melbourne, is now known as the Rod Laver Arena.

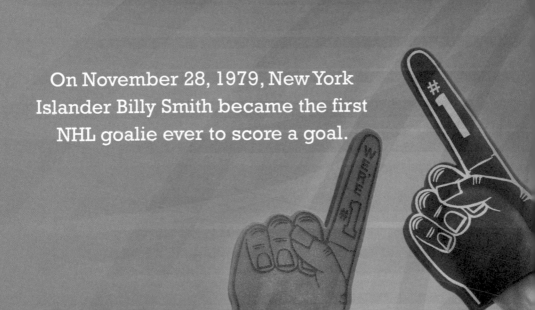

On November 28, 1979, New York Islander Billy Smith became the first NHL goalie ever to score a goal.

The Boston Celtics won the NBA championship
ten out of eleven seasons from 1958 to 1968.

Thirteen-year-old Alfred Hajos won two of the first four swimming events at the 1896 Athens Olympic games in the Bay of Zea's rough, 55-degree water.

Therefore, my beloved brothers, be steadfast,
immovable, always abounding in the work
of the Lord, knowing that in the Lord
your labor is not in vain.

1 Corinthians 15:58

In 1950, the Los Angeles Rams became the first NFL team to have all of its home and away games televised.

Only fifteen major leaguers have hit four home runs in one game. No player has ever done that during the postseason.

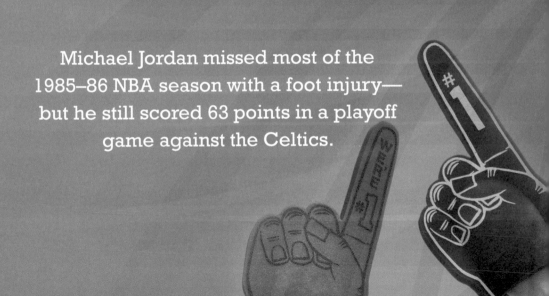

Michael Jordan missed most of the 1985–86 NBA season with a foot injury—but he still scored 63 points in a playoff game against the Celtics.

The LPGA is the longest-running independent women's professional sports organization, established in 1950 by thirteen founding members who not only played, but also organized tournaments and drafted rules.

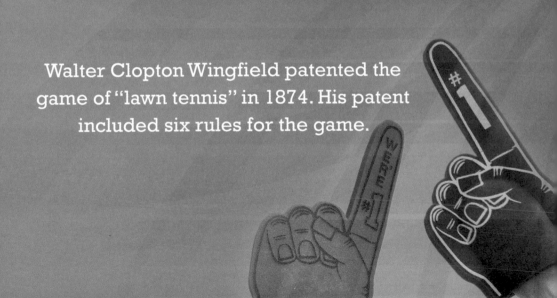

Walter Clopton Wingfield patented the game of "lawn tennis" in 1874. His patent included six rules for the game.

NASCAR claims seventy-five million fans nationwide and is now the second-highest rated sport on television—behind only the NFL.

After the rough swimming conditions of the 1896 Athens Olympics, the 1900 Paris games used the River Seine as a venue. Swimming with the current, contestants posted unusually fast times.

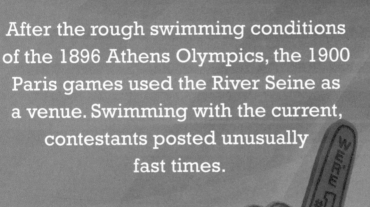

In 1952, the Pittsburgh Steelers became the last NFL team to abandon the single-wing formation in favor of the T-formation.

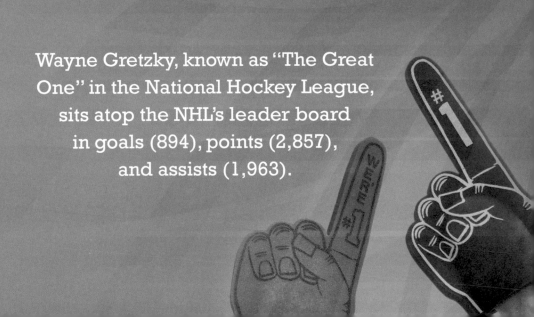

Wayne Gretzky, known as "The Great One" in the National Hockey League, sits atop the NHL's leader board in goals (894), points (2,857), and assists (1,963).

But I do not account my life of any value nor as precious to myself, if only I may finish my course and the ministry that I received from the Lord Jesus, to testify to the gospel of the grace of God.

ACTS 20:24

In 2001 at the Moon Valley Country Club in Phoenix, Annika Sorenstam shot 65-59-69-68 to go 27 under par—the LPGA's best round ever shot in relation to par for 72 holes.

The WNBA's all-time leading scorer is
Lisa Leslie, center for the Los Angeles Sparks.
Through 2008, she had 5,909 points.

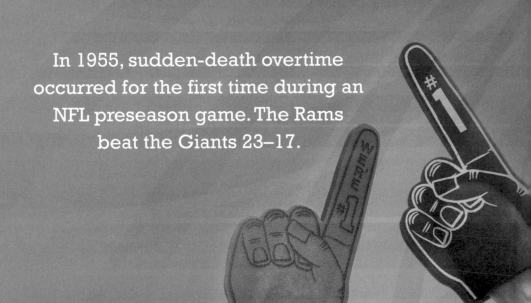

In 1955, sudden-death overtime occurred for the first time during an NFL preseason game. The Rams beat the Giants 23–17.

"Do you believe in miracles?" broadcaster Al Michaels shouted as the U.S. hockey team defied all odds, beating the heavily-favored Soviet team in the 1980 Lake Placid Olympics.

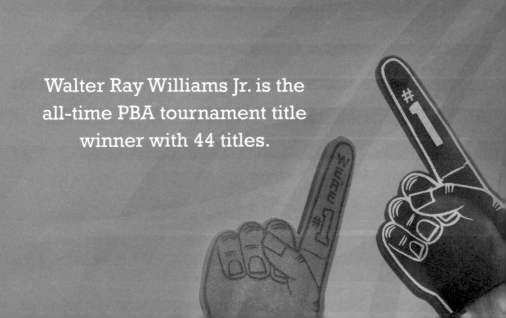

Walter Ray Williams Jr. is the all-time PBA tournament title winner with 44 titles.

Tennis player Don Budge became the first player to ever win the Grand Slam (all four major tournaments in one year) in 1938.

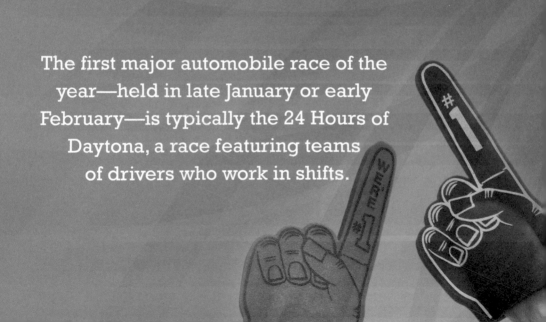

The first major automobile race of the year—held in late January or early February—is typically the 24 Hours of Daytona, a race featuring teams of drivers who work in shifts.

Women's soccer made its Olympic debut in Atlanta in 1996, as the United States defeated China 2–1 in the finals to win the gold medal.

Even though the Florida Marlins have twice won the World Series, they have never had a player hit for the cycle—a single, double, triple, and home run in a single game.

But they who wait for the L<small>ORD</small> shall renew their strength; they shall mount up with wings like eagles; they shall run and not be weary; they shall walk and not faint.

Isaiah 40:31

Metal tennis rackets gained favor in 1967, when Billie Jean King and Jimmie Connors begin using the Wilson T2000.

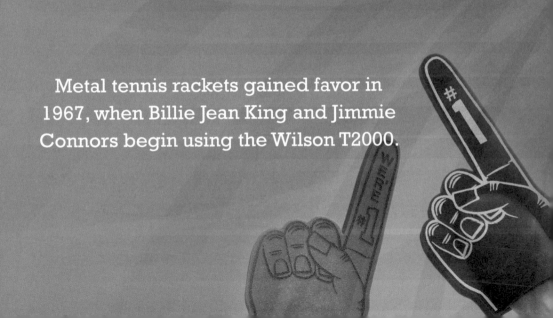

Richard Petty turned in one of NASCAR's best years ever in 1967, placing first in 27 of the 48 races he started, winning 10 in a row at one point.

Dave Ritchie scored the first goal in NHL history, just one minute into the first NHL game, December 19, 1917. Ritchie's Montreal Wanderers defeated the Toronto Arenas 10–9.

The NFL's all-time leading rusher is Emmitt Smith,
who spent the majority of his career with
the Dallas Cowboys. He gained 18,355
yards between 1990 and 2004.

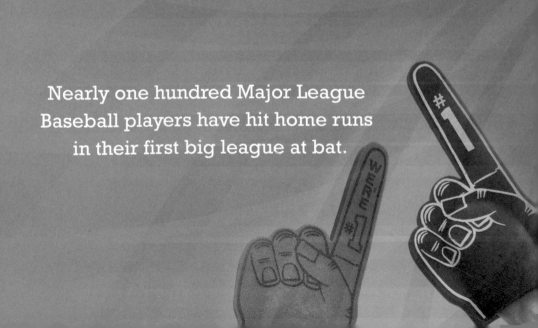

Nearly one hundred Major League Baseball players have hit home runs in their first big league at bat.

World War II caused the cancellation of the
1940 and 1944 Olympics—but a thirty-year-old
Dutch mother, Fanny Blankers-Koen, returned in
1948 to become the first woman to claim
four track-and-field gold medals.

The NBA's all-time leading scorer:
Kareem Abdul-Jabbar,
with 38,387 points.

Czechoslovakian runner Emil Zatopek,
in the 1952 Helsinki Olympics, became the
first (and only) runner to win the 5,000 meter,
10,000 meter, and the marathon races in
a single summer games.

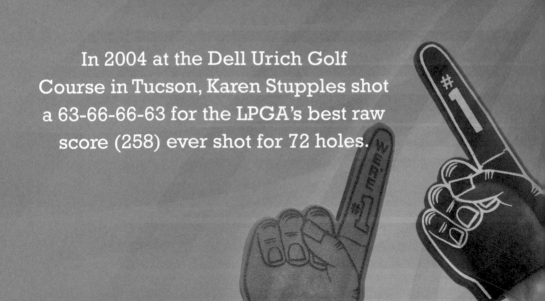

In 2004 at the Dell Urich Golf Course in Tucson, Karen Stupples shot a 63-66-66-63 for the LPGA's best raw score (258) ever shot for 72 holes.

. . .holding fast to the word of life, so that in the day of Christ I may be proud that I did not run in vain or labor in vain.

PHILIPPIANS 2:16

Babe Ruth's first Major League home run occurred on May 6, 1915, against New York Yankee pitcher Jack Warhop. Ruth played for Boston at the time.

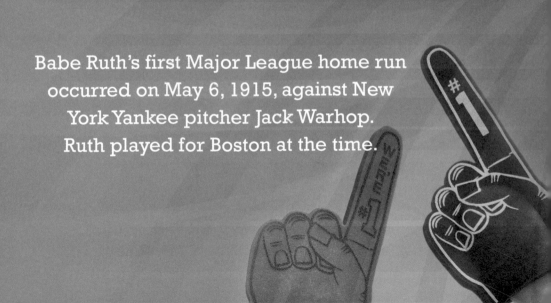

When Bobby Labonte won what is now known as the Sprint Cup in 2000, he and his brother Terry (who won twice) became the only championship-winning brothers in NASCAR history.

Through 2008, Brett Favre holds the NFL's all-time record for passing yards (61,655) and touchdowns (442).

Three drivers have won the Indianapolis 500 four times: A.J. Foyt (1961, '64, '67, '77); Al Unser (1970, '71, '78, '87); and Rick Mears (1979, '84, '88, '91).

U.S. Seniors Open competitor Mike Austin, age 64, drove a golf ball 515 yards in the 1974 championship held in Las Vegas. It's the longest drive ever recorded in a professional golf tournament.

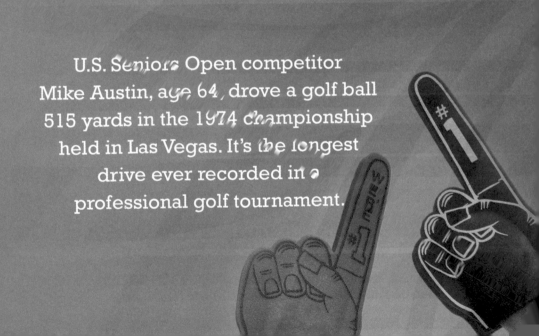

In 1968, the International Tennis Federation began the "Open Era" allowing professionals to play in major tennis tournaments.

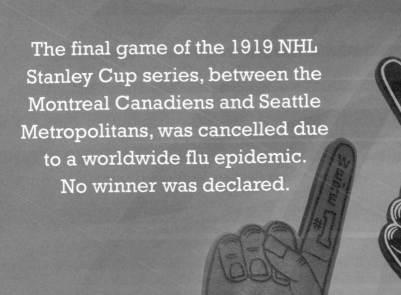

The final game of the 1919 NHL Stanley Cup series, between the Montreal Canadiens and Seattle Metropolitans, was cancelled due to a worldwide flu epidemic. No winner was declared.

The American Basketball Association (ABA), which operated from 1967 to 1976, was famous for using a red, white, and blue basketball.

U.S. gymnast Kerri Strug injured her ankle on her first vault in the 1996 Olympic team competition. Landing on one leg on her second vault, she helped the United States team win the gold medal.

And he is before all things,
and in him all things hold together.

COLOSSIANS 1:17

The NFL's all-time leader in field goals made is Morton Anderson, with 565 between 1982 and 2007.

Boston's Ted Williams hit .406 in 1941, the last major leaguer to bat better than .400 in a season.

In the 2007–08 season, NBA's tallest player was the Houston Rockets' Yao Ming, at 7 feet, 6 inches.

A hole-in-one on a par-five is sometimes referred to as a "condor." It can also be called a "triple-eagle" or a "double-albatross."

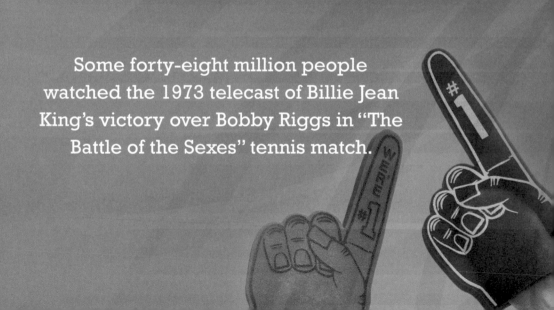

Some forty-eight million people watched the 1973 telecast of Billie Jean King's victory over Bobby Riggs in "The Battle of the Sexes" tennis match.

NASCAR driver Bill Elliot won the Most Popular Driver Award sixteen times—far more than any other competitor. He removed his name from consideration at the beginning of the 2003 season.